A RENEGADE'S RULES

A RENEGADE'S RULES

HOW A 'C' STUDENT CREATED AN 'A' LIFE, AND HOW YOU CAN, TOO

OLIVER SEIDLER

LIONCREST
PUBLISHING

A RENEGADE'S RULES

How a 'C' Student Created An 'A' Life, and How You Can, Too

ISBN   978-1-5445-0584-8 *Hardcover*

978-1-5445-0582-4 *Paperback*

978-1-5445-0583-1 *Ebook*

CONTENTS

PREFACE

I'm finishing this book, as crazy 2020 ends, but the pandemic is still going strong. It's such a powerful reminder that stuff is always going to happen. Well, there's also at least one more message there, and it's this: the way people respond *when* the worst happens is the true test of what they're made of. I'll tell you what separates the ones who succeed from those who don't—the ones who succeed respond *resiliently*.

So I have to ask you: how *much* do you want to make it, and how resilient are you willing to be to get there?

I ask because the pandemic has driven home still another message: life is too short to settle for anything less than you crave. It's time to go after it. *Now*.

If what you crave is to achieve success, you're in the absolute right book. And check this out: you can achieve that success even if you were a C student like me. Of course you don't *have* to have been a C student to get a lot out of the book, but if you were, it doesn't have to stop you. I'll go even further: I believe that being a C student might get you there *faster*, because you're willing to push harder than your former classmates who seemed to collect As just by breathing.

I want you to be well-rounded in every category of success: in your business and finances, of course; but also in your health (how you sleep, eat, and work out); in your relationships, both social and spiritual; and in your communities. The thing is, it takes financial success to craft that ideal life, so you can't ignore business and finance.

Let me be your guide on your journey to an all-around better life. I hope you can learn from some of my experiences. If you get even one insight or practice out of this book that moves you along your path to success, I'll be glad I wrote it.

I don't promise your journey will be easy. As you're about to see, mine sure wasn't. Like me, you'll have to crawl through the cracks, make your own mistakes, and deal with—*and bounce back from*—all the shit that happens in your life. When you do, you'll be at least halfway to where you want to be, because you'll have proved you have what it takes to make it. In that case, I expect you *will* make it.

Here we go.

INTRODUCTION

I was hungry. I'm still hungry.

The world is huge, and I want to make my mark on it.

Don't let the jeans and Converse sneakers fool you. The Rolex on my wrist won't tell you my story either. I might appear laid-back, but I'm burning inside.

I've built and rebuilt real estate businesses from the ground up—more than once. In my first job in real estate investing, we chased squatters and junkies from our properties. My boss smiled the first time he showed me the hand cannon strapped to his hip. Who carries a gun on a business deal? At that moment, I learned that this industry wasn't for the weak-minded or the timid. Assholes need not apply either.

My hunger comes from a dream. It comes from starting with nothing and using my own hands and brains and soul to create something. I made mistakes, and I paid the price. Throughout it all, I learned. I got better. I figured out a way to move forward, to excel, to blaze my own trail. It has been a journey, and it's not going to stop any time soon.

A PROUD C STUDENT

I say it all the time: Give me the C students who want to make something of themselves and aren't afraid of putting in the work. Give me someone average who will hit it hard every day, and I'll show you someone capable of incredible success.

I know this because I was that C student. I was never great in school—I just did what I needed to get by. Hell, I didn't even write this book entirely on my own; I got a ton of help in its creation.

In my twenties, I saw dudes with none of my drive or brains unrolling fat wads of cash, living it large. Seeing that ignited my hunger like a match to a flame. If they could do it, I sure as hell could do it too.

The only thing separating me from the life I wanted was the understanding that I was just as capable of success as any of those other guys. Figuring that out was life-changing.

Once I knew I could do it, I got up every day and hustled. Before long, the hustle started paying off, and I've never looked back.

UNDERSTANDING IS THE FIRST THING

When I got my first restaurant job, my dad warned me that it's easy to get sucked in. Bad work can be worse than having no job. At least without a job, you're looking for the next gig because you have to pay the rent. A bad job you're comfortable sticking with? That's just death.

Today, my life couldn't be further from the trail of unfulfilling restaurant jobs I left behind in my twenties. My business is successful. I've found the balance between working my ass off and taking time to enjoy what I've earned.

But the road hasn't always been smooth. My first job in real estate investment, in Pompano, Florida, looked more like the penny stock hothouse from the movie *Boiler Room* than the Century 21 office in a suburban strip mall that it was. But we'll get to that later. The point is, there have been endless challenges along the way, and I've had to hustle to get past every one of them.

I've started and sold multiple companies. I've fought with partners who, despite the battles, remain close friends (business can do that), and formed unbreakable bonds with others that last to this day. I've always focused on building a culture at my real estate investing company, PropertyForce. We give hardworking and hungry colleagues opportunities to build the lives they want, along with the holistic work-life balance to enjoy them.

I wrote this book to tell you how I did it.

P.T. BARNUM AND *THE GREATEST SHOWMAN*

Without a doubt, the movie that has affected me most in recent years was the Hugh Jackman musical *The Greatest Showman*. (Yeah, I know...a *musical*. But don't come at me—it's a great movie!) It tells the story of famed entrepreneur and entertainer P.T. Barnum, founder of the eponymous circus, which toured America for 148 years, from 1871 to 2017.

The real-life Barnum was a cool guy. In addition to founding the circus, he was a politician, who served in the Connecticut House of Representatives and as the mayor of Bridgeport. Barnum also wrote a ton of books and spent a lot of time calling bullshit on fortune tellers and mediums.

His career was all over the place, but he made it work.

The Greatest Showman tells the rags-to-riches story of Barnum's life. He came from nothing, married his childhood sweetheart, and eventually bought a wax museum that was almost out of money. Through force of will, Barnum turned this setup into one of the most successful circuses of all time.

Barnum wrestled with doubters and had huge setbacks— like the time his entire circus burned to the ground—and yet overcame all of it by taking risks and leaps of faith. Life is like that. It keeps knocking you on your ass to see if you'll get up. Success isn't about being the best. It's about resilience—getting back up no matter what happens.

Barnum lived enough highs and lows to fill several lives. As the movie also shows, he was human, so he let some of those setbacks get to him. He thought about stopping, about walking away. But he didn't. He always looked for a way to make it work.

Barnum's story moves me every time I watch the movie. You want to make your way in the world? You need someone to show you how to deal with the storms that life will throw your way? This is the movie to watch.

WHAT THIS BOOK IS

Today, I run a highly successful sales and marketing company that leverages technology to find real estate properties for investors. But that's not where I started—worried about making rent while I was chasing those squatters out of rotten houses in bad neighborhoods. How I got from there to here is quite the journey, and I wrote this book to show you what it looked like and the hard lessons it taught me. I wanted to share what's been tough for me and how I overcame it, in the hope that you can apply it to whatever goals you're going after in life.

Along the way, sure, we'll talk business; but this book isn't just for entrepreneurs or business owners. It's for anyone looking to live their dream. We'll follow my journey, and you'll follow the story of how I, a hungry guy with mediocre grades and a ton of street smarts, built an amazing life from the kinds of raw materials that the regular corporate world wouldn't know what to do with. Throughout my journey, I was propelled to success by three key drivers: openness to learning, willingness to take a leap of faith when needed, and the resilience to make it through whatever highs or lows life could throw at me.

The story will be entertaining and fun, while zooming in on an important message: the life you think is beyond your grasp is actually much closer than you think. It's a short story from different parts of my journey, followed by a simple lesson each part taught me.

If you can pick up even one lesson that helps you, the book will be a success. If it can go even further and teach you how to live a great life full of challenges—and also peace—I'll consider it a *home run*.

WHAT THIS BOOK IS NOT

This isn't a textbook. It wouldn't be, even if I knew how to write one. I'm also not standing at a lectern in front of you; we're just having a conversation. The act of writing has become a way for me to reflect on my own journey and how success is ultimately available to everyone. By getting this story down on paper and sharing it with you, I'm learning from my own experience; and I hope you learn from it too. That's the point of the book.

I don't claim to have all the answers. My teachers would say I had none of them! Frankly, I'm not even interested in answers in a larger sense. I'm looking for hustle, and the journey of figuring out the incremental answers as you go.

I'll tell you stories about how I found answers to problems as I encountered them. Your answers—and your mileage— may vary, so there would be no point in giving you a recipe. Instead, I'm doing a cooking demo because watching me cook *can* help. Welcome to my kitchen.

So let's jump in. To understand how I became the man I am, let's first look at the boy I was.

CHAPTER ONE

BEGINNINGS

Even though it was more than twenty-five years ago, I can still remember how it felt to sit on the floor of my dad's office and listen to him run his publishing business.

I remember the smell of the cigarette smoke wafting across his desk and the clicking sound of typewriters as my dad and Peter, his business partner, did their work. Sometimes they'd have long, involved discussions as they'd plan and strategize—often with a little cussing thrown in—or talk about their clients. I had a front-row seat to the operations of a successful business. You might think a little kid would be bored, but I absorbed everything I could.

Even as I grew into a teenager, that fascination never faded. My questions got smarter. I asked a lot of them, because I wanted to know how my dad made the decisions I watched him make. He was happy to answer them.

My dad also asked *me* questions. My favorite times were when he'd test my learning. "Okay, imagine you're the boss," he'd say, and describe a complicated problem. "What would you do?"

I'd put a lot of thought into my answer and propose a solution. Whether it was on-target or totally stupid, my dad would walk me through what he thought of it. Sometimes, I'd even hear the *best* possible response: "Guess what— that's exactly what we did."

Talk about a confidence booster. I basically had my own personal MBA program at my fingertips from the time I was old enough to read. When I look back on my own success, I know a huge part of it is how business is practically written into my DNA.

The biggest takeaway, though? *You've got to be resilient.*

You see, my dad wasn't always on top. He went from making tons of money to near bankruptcy many times throughout my childhood. The 1990s were especially tough on his business. One year, my brother and I would be living in a big house and going on vacations and to sleepaway camp; the next, we had downsized, and we spent the summer bussing tables.

The lesson I learned wasn't just what to do when you're on top—it was how to manage the bad times and climb back from the bottom.

My family knows that cycle of riches and ruin better than many, because it has followed that cycle for generations. To escape the Nazis, my Jewish grandfather moved to China. That's where my dad was born. After the war, they moved to England, where he met his future wife and my future mom. Her mother had escaped Nazi-controlled Poland, and her dad fought for the British in World War II. When they got married, my parents moved first to Canada, then to Miami in the late 1970s. In the early 80s, my brother and I were born there. All of that moving proves the adaptability of the people in my family. We roll with change and bounce back stronger.

I didn't realize how much that trait influenced my success until I started seeing other business colleagues experience extreme stress or even failure in the face of adversity. I've always reacted differently, more like: wow, this sucks; but hey, I'll just fix it.

I've always had a lot of confidence in my own adaptability. If there's anything I can count on, it's that I'll be able to figure things out!

My mother also did my brother and me the huge favor of

teaching us how money works. Unlike *so many* of our peers, we were never just handed things we wanted. It was made clear that we could have them if we paid for them with the one hundred dollars of allowance we each earned every month. We could divvy it up however we wanted, which we did on things like clothes, outside meals, and entertainment. My mom taught us how to create a budget and save.

I was a cheap kid! I loved figuring out how I could save the most. I saved as much as I possibly could. I built up a lot of money as a kid, not only from my allowance but from odd jobs I worked. What can I say? I was an entrepreneur in the making.

My mother's lessons would prove especially valuable later in life when I earned a lot more on my own. So would this one: as I was starting my first business, my dad's longtime business partner took me out to lunch. Where my dad was more the visionary, Peter had always had the more operational focus in the partnership.

He gave me this sound advice: "Oliver, don't ever be one of those guys who goes out and makes some money and blows it all on a Lamborghini right away. Don't be an idiot. Don't be flashy. You're going to have good times, but you're also going to have tough times. They come with any business. The people who can't endure those tough times drop out and leave behind market share for the people who stick it out. Which type of person are you going to be?"

In the years since, I've thought back on that moment a lot. He couldn't have been more right.

LESSON #1: RESILIENCE FIRST

How important is resilience? I'll tell you: it beats luck every time. That's the biggest lesson I learned growing up.

Most people who have enjoyed success in business didn't get there with luck. Sure, luck may give you a little boost from time to time, but consider it a nice-to-have, not a need-to-have.

Real success comes from a blend of working hard, taking risks, and having faith in your abilities.

That feast-or-famine cycle I watched my dad experience is a hallmark of business. It's going to happen—things are *not* going to be all sunshine and smooth sailing all the time. As Peter said, even if sometimes you could have enough money to pay cash for a Lamborghini, should you? *No*, because *you're* resilience-minded, so you know to save for a rainy day—the one when your luck changes again, as it inevitably will.

It's true what they say: luck favors the prepared. Part of what makes people truly resilient is being prepared for good times *and* bad.

Can you stay the course? Can you truly keep your hands on the wheel and drive forward, even when you're in the gutter? That's the mark of someone driving toward success. Scraping your way back from the bottom gives you the confidence you'll need to not only keep taking risks when you're at the top, but to feel safe knowing you'll always be able to bounce back when things dive again.

Here's my definition of the key to success: it's all about grit and being the last man standing. That might sound simple, but it isn't easy to do; it means enduring a lot of bad times, self-doubt, betrayals, market changes, and any number of other bad breaks.

Hell, *my* very first attempt to "make it" as an adult ended up badly. I was poor, pissed off, and heading home to Florida with my tail between my legs. You'll read that story in the next chapter. I went after what I thought my ideal life would be, and I took a body blow. I had to totally change direction.

But I didn't lose my hunger. I'd been knocked down, but if I knew anything, it was that I could always get up again. That confidence, that resilience, is what makes an entrepreneur. Without it, you're just a guy with a dream. So stay strong,

stay hungry, and keep your head down. Work through whatever comes!

CHAPTER TWO

FINDING MY DIRECTION

When I said that I'm hungry, I wasn't fucking around. Sometimes I think I came into this *world* hungry.

When I was a kid, this hunger came out in the number of jobs I had, most of them in foodservice and retail. No gig was beneath me; I wanted the freedom of a paycheck, and from the time I was thirteen years old, I worked. First I was a busboy earning sixty-five dollars a week. Other early jobs included gas station attendant, Baskin Robbins scooper, pizza-delivery driver, and telemarketer.

All through college, I worked in restaurants from fast-casual to fine-dining and everything in between. By the end of college, if I could claim any real expertise in the job market, it was restaurants that handed it to me. I learned a lot about how to talk to people, find out what they want to hear, and give them a great experience, even if all they ordered was an appetizer and a glass of water. It also helped me get over my shyness, which helped with my future public speaking, because I *had* to talk to people, to whomever was sitting in my section.

My employment in restaurants was also a masterclass in humility, because I would not have chosen to talk to some of those people in any other circumstances. The humility lesson, of course, was serving people—taking care of them no matter how they treated me. And many of them treated me like crap.

Along with the restaurant work, I was finally finishing up my last semester. Most of my friends had graduated in four years and had moved on by then. It had taken *me* five and a half. So, without my buddies around, I decide to move to Los Angeles to chase my dreams.

Unfortunately, every aspiring actor and model on the planet had the same idea. I couldn't get a job as a server at any restaurant in the city. One day, a restaurant manager who happened to be from near my South Florida hometown took pity on me and offered me a hosting job. It was at a well-known, trendy little bistro in Hollywood, frequented by actors and industry folk. I couldn't have cared less about meeting them, but the job came with at least one cool perk: my coworker up at the host stand was a swimsuit model.

It was fun, but it paid only about half my bills. I landed a second gig as a food runner at an old-school fine-dining restaurant. It was the worst job I've ever had. I was carrying back-breaking trays and getting screamed at by the head chef at every turn.

With both jobs combined, I was working for barely minimum wage, while sharing a shitty one-bedroom overlooking drug dealers on Sunset Strip. At every turn, I was painfully aware of the other end of the lifestyle spectrum. Beverly Hills was right down the road from me. The heights of opulence were at my fingertips, but I couldn't even get close enough to touch.

For a guy as hungry as me, this was basically torture.

The thing is, I'd had a taste of the luxe life. In my first year of college, my dad had sold his Florida business and moved out to Beverly Hills, where I'd often visited him. Money flowed like a river out there. I got used to driving in the nicest cars, eating in the nicest restaurants, and living large in the country's most expensive zip code. Not just *used* to it—I *loved* it. It was part of the reason I moved to LA a few years later. I was chasing that same high, trying to build for myself that same no-limits dream. I wanted that life back.

But the reality of LA was kicking my ass.

All through college, when people had asked me what I wanted to do with my degree, I answered without hesitation: "I'm going to be rich. I'm going to build my own business." I knew I wanted what my dad had finally achieved, after a life of struggle, and that it was possible.

At one point, my dad had a birthday dinner at the fine-dining restaurant where I worked, which gave me a taste of things on the other side of the table. I found myself spilling out my goals to one of his friends, a successful surgeon: "I'm going to be rich; I'm going to be super successful," the usual story. He listened patiently, for a bit, and then stopped me.

"Listen," he said. "I came from the Bronx. I had no money at all. I had to work for where I'm at, in tiny incremental steps, and it felt like it was taking forever to get to where I wanted to be.

"But now I'm here. And I look at people who make all their money and get successful right away—actors, sports stars, rock stars—and they don't know what to do with that much success at once. They didn't work hard or long enough for it. They turn to drugs, alcohol, sex, all kinds of stuff, because they're chasing that high. So here's my advice to you: don't be in such a rush to conquer the world. Work hard, be the best at everything you do, and be cool with getting there incrementally, step by step."

It seemed like good advice, and I took it to heart. But at the same time, I had been certain that moving to LA was my ticket to *making it*. So far, I'd made next to no money, I missed my friends back home, and I felt like the smallest fish in the biggest pond in the world. It was a rude awakening and a big part of the growing up I did in my twenties. Some people dive into the LA scene and feel right at home. Others, like me, are never able to find their direction or sense of place.

Relationships felt artificial and transactional; I was hustling hard and seeing no results. It was all about *who you know*, and I didn't know anybody.

I wasn't alone. I watched every aspiring young actor who'd beat me out for serving jobs—kids who'd been the best-looking people in their small towns—get rejection served to them on a plate day after day.

Opportunities were scarce. I decided I could never envision myself building a life out there.

So, shortly after it began, my West Coast adventure came to an end. I packed up what little I owned and bought a one-way ticket back to South Florida.

In Florida, I fell right back into my old niche: the service industry. I got a job at a high-end restaurant. I was making money, but I wasn't working toward anything I cared about. I'd have killed for that kind of job in LA, and it could make me a comfortable living for several twenty-something years. But I was completely unfulfilled.

Day after day, I'd watch guys who looked *just* like me waltz in and spend more on a single lunch than I took home in a week's tips. Booze, steaks, the whole spread. They didn't have to think twice about the cost. They'd entertain clients, close deals, and build businesses, and I could only clear their plates and watch. It was a punch in the gut.

I'll never forget the day I watched a guy who couldn't have been five years older than me order round after round of top-shelf tequila for a table of clients. I kept bringing over the trays of shots, friendly and smiling, but inside, I was burning. *This guy isn't smarter than me. He isn't funnier or more charming. He's nothing special.*

The only difference between us was that I was waiting tables and he was living my dream.

I knew, then and there, that I had to get out of serving. I'd been putting my time into serving other people since I was thirteen years old. I was done.

I wanted *more*.

I was about to take a leap of faith. As I said before, I was confident in my resilience and ability to adapt. I knew I would be able to take a risk because I knew I'd be able to take care of myself no matter how it turned out.

Opportunity was ripe; this was 2004, and real estate was hot, especially in South Florida. A buddy of mine took me out for drinks, one night, and started raving about the tons of money his company was making by buying and selling distressed properties.

"It's a free-for-all," he told me, clinking his beer bottle against mine. "There's room for everybody, and we're all getting rich."

Jackpot.

I finally had a concrete goal to attack. The next day, I quit my restaurant job. I walked out that door, knowing I was walking toward something more.

LESSON #2: NO MATTER WHAT YOU'RE DOING, BE THE BEST

I moved to LA, absolutely certain it was my ticket to getting rich. All it ended up being was a ticket back to Florida. But while I was there, I learned two valuable lessons: first, no matter what work you're doing, make it your mission to be the best at it and to make the most of every opportunity. I didn't like a lot of my jobs or even most of them, but I sucked it up and worked hard, so I could be better than the guy next to me and earn praise from my bosses and customers. The competitive edge and recognition feel good and set you up for bigger things down the road. You might not be working your dream job, but you're still practicing and embodying the ability to be your best, so you'll have it when it really matters.

Here's the second lesson I learned: part of being the best is not wasting time grinding yourself into dust, trying to make something work that just doesn't. Know when it's time to cash in your chips and move on.

Sometimes you're going in the wrong direction. Hey, it happens to all of us, and that's fine. But you have to be able to recognize when it's wrong and course-correct. Otherwise, you're the guy who follows his GPS instead of his eyes and drives his car into a river.

When I got to LA, I was sure I was going to make it, and I was totally game for paying my dues, doing my time, and working my way up the ladder. I didn't lack any work ethic; that was for sure. But it took me a while to realize that there *was* no ladder. I thought I just had to learn how to play the game. It turns out that the rules weren't set up for people like me to win. And every other big fish from a small pond was out there with me, trying to be the winner.

The best thing I ever did was change direction and leave the game to them. Let them bang their heads against a wall, year after year. I knew there were better opportunities elsewhere, and thankfully, I wasn't so attached to my dream of "making it" that I didn't know when to quit.

It took even more humility than I had learned in my early restaurant jobs, and I had to learn it. Once I did, I got out, and I urge you to do the same. Don't let pride get in the way of your success.

Be the best, and know when the answer isn't to work harder. Make sure you're going the right—best—way. Your road isn't predetermined. *You* get to decide which direction you drive and how you drive. How should you drive? Like the best.

CHAPTER THREE

LEARNING THE ROPES

I never said I went from waiting tables to a million-dollar business in a day. Hell, it took a while to go from waiting tables to even having an *idea* of the kind of business I might want to build.

My first, biggest problem was cash flow—quitting the restaurant had given me both the time and the motivation to pursue business ideas, but I'd eaten through my meager savings. I knew I had to get another pay-the-rent job. I also had to keep my days clear, though, to dive into real estate. It was a tall order.

I managed to find a job at the *one* nightclub in Boca Raton. Luck was on my side—hell, maybe I was owed a little luck after how bad LA had been to me.

So my new normal began. I got my real estate license and, by day, I got that job selling investment real estate I told you about. By night I was a bouncer at the nightclub. Most of the time I averaged about three hours of jittery sleep. The minute my alarm went off, I launched out of bed, slammed down about a gallon of coffee from the gas station across the street, and put everything I had into showing and selling properties. By the time 6:00 p.m. rolled around, I had just enough energy left to throw on my nightclub uniform (black -shirt, take-no-shit attitude) and get to the club. I'd be home by 4:00 a.m., and the whole thing started over the next morning.

Complicating matters was my roommate situation. When I was a teenager, I smoked a lot of weed. I stopped smoking when I moved to LA, but all my old friends in Florida were still in that scene. They included the guys whose house I moved into, except by then, they had graduated from weed to ecstasy, cocaine, and other hard drugs. Most nights I'd get home in the early hours of the morning only to find them still awake partying, and it was hell trying to get some sleep. There was a silver lining to being there, though. It provided constant motivation to make money so I could find a better place to live.

I didn't care that I was probably shaving years off the back end of my life. I was determined. I knew, beyond a shadow of a doubt, that I was going to make it in sales and investment real estate. This was my *shot*. I had to give it every ounce of hunger I'd built up. I had to put my head down and sacrifice. I had to *hustle*. If I could do that, *I* would be the one buying clients fancy lunches in no time. Screw that, I'd be the client *other people* wined and dined.

But at the end of that first month, I counted up my earnings, and after subtracting gas money and overhead...I'd made a grand total of *nothing*.

I gritted my teeth, drained my last drop of savings to make rent, and threw myself into the next month. Turns out, that was my learning month. And the second month? That was my *earning* month.

With all my hard work, I'd built a solid foundation of knowledge: how to find the right clients, the right way to talk to them, and the steps to take to close deals. I also built a map in my head of every corner in South Florida, and I knew the pulse of the area well. In that second month, it felt like I did *everything* right and it all came together. By the end of the month, I'd made $10,000. I moved out of the party house I was living in, and I quit my job at the club.

That was the last pay-the-rent job I'd ever have.

LESSON #3: YOUR PAST DOESN'T DEFINE YOUR FUTURE

This was a big pivot point in my life. I had moved away from the industry I'd always worked in—restaurants—and put everything I had into breaking into a new business. I saved every penny that came my way so that I could leave behind my old druggie friends and become the man I wanted to be.

It worked out, and it taught me a big lesson: you can make your future whatever you want it to be. You don't have to be defined by your past.

You can pivot to whatever future you imagine for yourself. It involves taking a risk, but no life worth having is without risk.

No business, job, or career worth having comes without risk either. If there's no risk, you know what a risk-free business is called? A *paycheck*. A lot of people go to work for someone else in order to avoid taking on risk. But you can also work for someone else, doing something you're passionate about and that rewards you—if you're willing to risk it.

Of course my cushy restaurant gig was risk-free. But the first big risk I took as an entrepreneur happened way before I actually opened my business: it was the day I walked out of that restaurant gig without a safety net or a plan.

It took me being filled with hunger and confronted with

the life I wanted, but wasn't living, to take that important leap of faith.

Tons of people never take that leap because they feel defined by their past. They don't know anything else. They tell themselves, "I can't do that—I don't know how. I only know how to do what I've done." That's a limiting belief. It holds so many people back from leaping toward something better.

I'll be honest; I was never actually all that good at waiting tables. For one thing, my memory isn't great (all that weed I smoked as a teenager), and the job requires you to remember which table needs what. The other problem was that I only faked the confidence and self-assurance I exhibited there.

As soon as I switched to real estate, though, that confidence became real. Looking back on that first $10,000 month, I know I got there because I thought: *yes! I can do this!* That level of success catapulted the faith I had in myself, but that faith was already there. It had been all along—I just needed to find the right outlet to be able to access it.

Being an entrepreneur won't work if you don't have that ability to jump off the ledge, certain of your ability to build the parachute on the way down. Of course, playing it safe works great for many people who find happiness in a life of caution.

But caution isn't for me. Because you're still reading this, I suspect it isn't for you either.

Get comfortable with risk! Make a change and take massive action towards it, with the confidence that, no matter what happened in your past, you can go a *lot* further than you've been thinking you can. I know that for two reasons. The first is that you're better than you think you are. You have everything inside you that you need to succeed if you trust that you do. The second reason is you're living in America, the land of opportunity. Make and grab the opportunity to leave behind your past, and go after the future you've imagined.

CHAPTER FOUR

BANDITS

When the hours I'd spent learning the ropes finally started to pay off at the new job, I was beyond excited. Never again would I have to put on a server's uniform. Never again would I have to bounce around town, from gig to gig, and crawl into bed exhausted at the crack of dawn. Never again would I have to wonder where the hell my rent was coming from.

I was *set*. The good days had finally arrived! I was so pumped that, at first, I didn't notice the mess of a company I'd unintentionally stumbled into.

It only took me a couple of months to figure out that the company's method of selling real estate was ruthless, dirty, and every man for himself.

The guys working at the company were professional hustlers, but not in the positive sense of the word. I was one of them—for a couple of years at least. The aggression in the office was something you could see and literally touch, down to the wrestling matches we'd hold when the boss left for the day. One guy from Pennsylvania, a former Penn State wrestler who was missing a front tooth, could slam anyone to the ground in less than five seconds, and he did it to huge cheers. It was that kind of place.

On my first day at the job, my new boss and I headed out to visit some of the firm's properties. I don't know what I expected from the real estate business, but I definitely did *not* expect to find myself knocking on doors in one of Miami's worst neighborhoods. Outside the first run-down, boxy, cement-patched house, I felt confused.

"We're going to go in here?" I asked, as the sounds of someone yelling obscenities came muffled through the door.

My boss, all five-feet-eight-inches of him, smiled and pulled up the hem of his untucked shirt. A massive nickel-plated .357 Magnum Revolver stuck out from the waistband of his pants. "Don't worry about it," he told me.

Inside was your basic shit show. Squatters had taken over the house for what looked like at least a few months. A man sat on the floor, eating SpaghettiOs straight from the can and watching a four-inch TV that looked like it had been through a few wrestling matches itself. The whole back of the house was flooded out, and in one of those rooms, we found a woman sleeping on a bare mattress. The plumbing didn't work, and you know the place smelled horrendous.

These were the properties we were going to sell?

Yes. After we cleared out the squatters and secured the place, my boss had me plant an "Investment Opportunity" sign with our contact info on the raggedy lawn. We put up these "bandit signs," as we called them, all over the neighborhood.

Every time we pulled up to a spot and I jumped out of the car with a sign, groups of locals on the street corners would stare like I was about to get a beatdown. It was obvious that we were intruders on their turf, but my boss didn't seem to care. Meanwhile, I found myself wondering if anyone had ever been killed on the job and if my boss would even tell me if they had.

The signs totally worked. The system my boss taught me pretty much boiled down to planting seeds in the morning and then harvesting all afternoon as I fielded calls from investors. In hindsight, the difference between the two halves of the day was hilarious: mornings spent crawling through windows and dodging gangbangers in the most dangerous neighborhoods in South Florida; and afternoons spent at a desk, taking calls like any normal office job.

All fifteen of us who worked in inside sales were in our twenties, looking to make as much money as we could. And we did—we made a ton. It was a big step up from my days slinging drinks.

LESSON #4: COMMIT 100%

The lesson I want you to take away from my early days in investment real estate is *not* that you have to be willing to get shot up to succeed. And actually, the circumstances of where I was working, what kinds of crazy shit we did to make money, and the atmosphere the guys created in the office are totally irrelevant to the lesson here. (Makes for a good story though, and I love scaring new guys with the tales of my early years.)

The big takeaway is that I could have been selling *anything*—stocks, vacuum cleaners, insurance, whatever—and the principles I used to succeed would be the same.

First, I committed myself 100 percent to what I was doing. I learned my boss's system, I followed the steps he set up perfectly, and I was *consistent*—that's important—and allowed the results to follow. I stuck with it, even when the system seemed to be working more slowly than I would have liked.

Second, I used whatever extra time I had to learn from guys who'd been successful for a long time. I was "modeling the masters," to borrow a phrase. I didn't feel the need to waste a single second trying to reinvent the wheel; I just went to those in the know and asked them to teach me.

I'd imagined so many different ways I'd go after my dreams of being rich and successful, but right out of college, I'd had a bucket of cold water thrown over me—getting rich had been a *lot* harder than I'd thought it would be. But working in a commission-only environment in investment real estate showed me that—if I worked hard, opened myself up to learning, and committed—I could get good at something. As I mentioned, this was the first time in my career when I gained true confidence in what I was doing, so I started to excel beyond just *good*. In my first year, I made $100,000 and was in the top ten out of 150 salesmen at the company. In a single month, on my anniversary of joining the company, I made $30,000.

I learned that I had a knack for sales. I learned that I was truly good at something. It built an incredible amount of confidence, and that confidence gave me momentum in going after even bigger things.

My frugal ways from childhood—the lessons my mom had taught me about budgeting—paid off big-time at this point. I was making more money than I'd ever seen in my life, and I wasn't blowing it all on cars and fancy nights out. I'd taken to heart the advice my dad's business partner gave me: "Save for a rainy day because sometimes you're up, but you can also get knocked back down."

When you're getting started in your career, opportunities aren't going to look all tied up in a beautiful ribbon. Sometimes they're going to look a little like a scam. That doesn't mean they're bad. *Any* opportunity can be a good one if you throw yourself into it completely, follow the steps you're given by people who know what they're doing, stay consistent (which is *mandatory* for reaching real success), and learn as much as you can. Using that mindset, you can literally make money doing anything.

CHAPTER FIVE

BREAKING OUT

My real estate job taught me a lot about learning a system and committing myself to learning, but the learning had a definite downside (or, I guess in the end, an upside): I started seeing the red flags. First it was a couple, here and there. As I grew my base of knowledge, I came to understand that I was working inside a house of cards.

There's no other way to really look at it: their business practices were straight-up unethical. You may have seen a movie called *The Big Short*, in which lenders were selling loans to people who had absolutely no business taking on the debt. The finance department at my company was even deeper down the rabbit hole; they had appraisers value houses for more than they were actually worth. So when the market started to crash, the borrowers, who had rotten credit, stopped paying off the loans. Then the old, wealthy guys who had bought the loans from our company were left holding a bag of underwater, upside-down shit.

It's no wonder the housing market went belly-up a couple years later. But that's a later story.

I stayed on at that company for longer than I should have, eventually becoming their top salesman. One day, word came down that they wanted me to move to a new city to open a new branch office.

The speed at which I rejected the idea and the level of immediate disgust I felt at the thought were like wake-up calls for my conscience. It was obvious that I was *not* okay with the company anymore. There was no way I could keep working there. It was time to go. I turned over all my business contacts and left.

About a year later, the company folded, which showed that my instinct to leave was right. It also showed that ethical practices always prevail in the long run. (What it doesn't show, and what I'm *not* suggesting, is that my absence immediately caused the whole company to tank!)

Now right around the time I was getting cold feet at the real estate "boiler room," I'd started to work on a side hustle: with my accountant friend Jason I bought a big house in Pompano, Florida, to remodel and flip. We had planned to spend about $30,000 in repairs before selling. As with anything that's related to real estate, though, that number ended up bloating. By the time we were done, we'd put in almost $80,000 of our own money.

It was a huge risk, but a calculated one. We weren't first timers looking to get rich quick. We both had the base of expertise needed to actually succeed at a house-flipping venture—real estate in my case and accounting in his. And succeed we did: we earned a tidy profit once we sold the property.

More importantly, though, we realized that we worked well together. We had great chemistry and mutual trust. We had complementary skills and were both looking for a job change. So, buoyed by our successful collaboration on the house, and with the future wide open, we knew it was time to make our move. We decided to pool our resources and go into business for ourselves.

In 2006, Jason and I opened Meridian Trust LLC. In many ways, this was a dream come true: *finally!* At last I was cashing the check I'd written over and over when I was younger and swore to people that I was going to own a business. I felt like I was coming into my own.

At first, we worked out of the tiny bedroom of my Fort Lauderdale apartment. Then, as soon as possible, we moved into the nicest office space we could afford. From the jump, we were focused on doing things the right way, which to us meant starting out small and bootstrapped—no investors, no loans, no help whatsoever. Each of us put up $15,000, and we grew organically from there.

This route may have made those first few years a little tougher on us; but we liked the challenge, and we had confidence in each other's unique perspective and abilities. Jason knew about numbers, and I knew about real estate. He was an operations guy, and I was more about the vision and sales. He wasn't interested in climbing the corporate ladder, and I wasn't interested in making unethical deals.

Most importantly, we both had incredible work ethic, we were both hungry, and we were both willing to hustle. In those early days, whatever it took to get the job done—again, ethically—is what we would do.

LESSON #5: LIVE THE FUTURE YOU'RE TRYING TO CREATE

When Jason and I started Meridian, it felt a little like fake it 'till you make it. But that's not the lesson I want you to take away from that story, because we really weren't faking it. We had the experience, skills, and proven track record to know we were on the right track.

What helped us out was committing to our future vision and living into it as much and as soon as possible. We could have worked out of my apartment bedroom for a hell of a lot longer, and we'd have taken home way more cash. But somehow we both knew deep down that *looking* and *feeling* serious meant we *were* serious. That's why we quickly put money into upgrading our work environment.

It's not as if the space was big. In fact, at seventy-nine square feet, it was tiny—the smallest office in the building. But the *building* was the nicest one in town. When we, a couple of twenty-five-year-olds, walked into that building, at first we didn't feel like we belonged there. But instead of wanting to fit in with the stream of well-dressed law-yers and wealth managers who worked there, we wanted to beat them. That attitude fueled us in kind of a perverse way. Instead of wearing suits as they did, we dressed cool and casual, wanting to look like the scrubbiest people in the elevator—but the ones who were making the most money. We still dress that way; it boosted our confidence, our sense of being taken seriously. That feeling carried over into our interactions with clients. We looked important, and it made us *feel* important, which made our prospective clients also see us that way and trust us with their business.

None of this was without risk. In fact, this was probably the riskiest time in my early career. I'd left a job, where I'd made $250,000 by the age of twenty-four, to start my own company. Jason had been on the partner track at his accounting firm. We were both comfortable and headed to even greater heights. And yet we chose to leave it all behind, put all our savings into an investment, and make it on our own. We were confident, and we were resilient, and we knew the truth that's worth repeating: there's no avoiding risk when it comes to living into the future you want.

When you're trying to make something happen, it's important to live into every piece of it fully. Let the bootstrapping happen in the background—in your bank account. Call it faking it 'till you make it if you want, but whatever you call it, it *works*: present a successful front, and you're more likely to be treated like a success. That effect tends to multiply.

If you step up the reality around you, you will start leveling up to it. That also applies to the various players in your life story. As Stephen Covey has written, you naturally become the five people you surround yourself with most often. That's why I *had* to leave my former roommates. I could not change my reality until I changed my environment.

Although Jason and I didn't want to model ourselves exactly on our neighbors in the new office building, we did appreciate and covet their success. Well, we craved *greater* success than they had, and the daily exposure to their success helped to drive us to achieve our own. I even question if we would have survived the real estate crash (coming in the next chapter) if we hadn't leveled up when, and to the extent, that we did.

CHAPTER SIX

CRASH

In 2006, when Jason and I started Meridian, the market was already showing signs of trouble. Homes had stopped increasing in value, mortgage delinquencies had started to rise, and homeowners had stopped selling. With the fall of the subprime market, in July of the following year, the "bubble" turned into a full-blown crisis.

The housing market had essentially collapsed, and banks were freezing most, if not all, lending. In that difficult environment, we struggled to find buyers and put together deals. The year before, Jason and I had hired two assistants and a couple junior sales agents. We moved all of our desks into a 400-square-foot room that we called the "war room." From that room, we fought tirelessly. We fought to find the right properties. We fought to get banks to loan us money. We fought to get investors to close. Prices were constantly changing—usually downward, falling as fast as they had risen in the previous years.

Every day was a surprise. Every day was stressful. Every day was a *battle*.

In the front of the office, we had a whiteboard where we listed all of our active and pending deals—when we *had* any. The board stayed essentially empty, day in and day out, and it got almost depressing after a while. Deals that did make the board stayed on it forever.

It was a desperate time. There was a lot of yelling. It was hard to hang on to our positivity and confidence when there was just *no money* coming in. Sometimes we found ourselves cursing people out on the phone—I had flashbacks to the boiler room, a place I never wanted to go back to. Investors and banks were backing out of deals, and we couldn't close; and that meant we couldn't capture revenue we needed to pay our bills.

Day after day, we held out hope that the investors would come back. Day after day, we were disappointed.

And the ones who *did* show up often treated us like shit.

One deal in particular sticks out in my mind. We were going to make a $10,000 fee if it closed, and we went after it *hard*.

The investor knew he was one of only five in town doing this kind of deal. Knowing we didn't have a choice, he strung us along. He had all the power and all the leverage, and in the end he played us—he backed out, and we didn't make a penny. It was *brutal* to have spent all that time and *begged* him to close, only to have us once again faced with a zero.

By 2008, we started to run out of money.

Coming into the office each day was like getting punched in the face. More than once, Jason or I said, "If this deal doesn't happen—if this doesn't happen *today*—we're dead." One day he'd want to quit, and the next day I'd want to. If we hadn't been so resilient, we would have done it. We also had to lean on each other a lot and hold onto hope. The best way we could stay sane was to insist each of us take a vacation, with money we definitely shouldn't be spending; it was either that or our sanity.

Bear Sterns collapsed during Jason's vacation. I called him and said, "It's really bad. Everything's crashing. The economy is going down the tubes."

It turned out we had not chosen the best time to start a real estate investment firm.

Every one of our competitors went out of business that year. We didn't, all because we held onto one important rule:

don't buy a house to remodel and resell unless you know you can rent it for a decent amount if you have to. If you can't cover your expenses with the rent you can make on that house afterward, do not buy it.

That, of course, is because sometimes the house just doesn't sell.

Let's run through the numbers to show you exactly why this rule matters. Say you buy a house for $70,000, and you put $10,000 into it and can resell it for $110,000. When the deal closes and all commissions and closing costs are figured, you'll make about $20,000. But if the market turns and you can't sell it, you have to be able to rent it out to cover mortgage, taxes, and insurance—and, ideally, make a small return.

If you can rent that house out for between $1,100 and $1,300, you're okay because you're still getting a decent return on your investment, and you can sell the property when demand returns and prices climb. If you can only rent it for $700, you're screwed. Every month you send more money out the door than you can make back.

If the house doesn't make rental sense, you will go bankrupt—whether quickly or slowly—the second the market turns against you. It's inevitable. In 2007 and 2008, that's exactly what happened to a lot of people: when the market turned and their properties couldn't make enough rent, they folded.

These people were buying houses for even bigger numbers than in the scenario I laid out above. More expensive houses also had higher mortgages and property taxes, even though their neighborhoods couldn't support rents that were high enough to cover the costs.

Rents don't go up nearly as fast as purchase costs. That means the people—our competitors—who were in the worst shape were the ones who bought homes for $300,000. They had thought they would be able to fix them up and sell them for $450,000. But they ended up paying four times as much to make only 20 percent more in rent, and it crippled them.

When the bottom fell out of the market, they were left holding *tons* of inventory. It cost them everything.

But because Jason and I had the foresight to never close on a house and hold it as inventory, unless the house made sense as a rental, we were one of the few companies left standing when the market crashed.

LESSON #6: DON'T PANIC! TRUST YOUR SYSTEMS

We kept coming back to work, fighting battle after battle to stay in the game, for a few key reasons.

One was that we had been really cocky when we started the business. We'd talked smack to all our friends, telling them, when we first started making money, how we were going to be millionaires. If we gave up, we'd have to tell them we'd messed up—that we'd *failed*.

For the sake of our egos alone, failure for us wasn't an option. But we also had employees who depended on us, and Jason and I had both left our jobs to start this business. While my partner may have had a job to return to, I certainly didn't.

Our recovery wasn't just luck. Jason and I had solid systems in place for when people were getting back into investing, and when they started coming back around, we were ready for them. It took some creativity, but we were able to dig our way back up after waiting out the storm.

By the middle of 2009, homes that had been selling for $170,000 were now selling for $50,000. With prices so low, it didn't matter if we couldn't resell them; we could fix them up and rent them out easily, earning ourselves a tidy 20–25 percent return in the process.

So that's exactly what we did.

We weren't the only ones to see the opportunity. Soon private investors started coming back for the rental market investment returns. Then the institutional investors showed up and began buying in bulk. Suddenly we had no trouble reselling the houses we had acquired. The market picked up, and our business bounced back.

We recovered, but we never forgot the lessons we learned during the so-called Great Recession. No matter how good things get, the situation can always take a turn for the worse—and quickly. I still remember what it was like in the war room, fighting for our very survival every day. But we didn't panic; we stuck with our systems and stayed the course. Every day we would come into the office and just try to do the right thing.

These days, if we have a bad quarter, I only have to think back to how we got through the 2007–2009 recession. That keeps me from freaking out too much. Because we weathered that crazy downturn, I'm confident that we can weather anything the market throws at us. We know that above all else, we got through it because we trusted our systems—and didn't flail around when things got bad.

But I can't say everyone has learned those lessons. Only a decade or so later, I see people every day who forget how bad it was in 2008. They forget about their neighbors who lost their houses and their jobs. So they're getting into real estate again and buying and fixing up houses without worrying whether they're rent-worthy. They're also buying those new cars that my father's old partner warned me against, because they think they're invincible.

As I write this, the market is up, but I know it won't be forever. Even in the best times, you still need discipline and patience.

As Jason, my business partner, once told me, "Pigs get fat; hogs get slaughtered."

Too much greed is a recipe for disaster in any field. But in real estate, it's actually toxic.

As you've seen in this chapter, the lesson here is to follow best practices of real estate investment. But as the chapter also shows, what's at least as important is sticking to your principles and morals. Even when we were getting screwed left and right, we always took the high road and did business on the up-and-up. We also knew to keep showing up—coming into the office every day and working through whatever came. Once again, we proved the power of resilience. This left us with a good reputation and even greater confidence that we could survive the harshest conditions.

CHAPTER SEVEN

SEIZING OPPORTUNITY

After the worst effects of the crash had died away and Meridian Trust was recovering well, Jason and I found ourselves able to stop and take a breath for the first time in a couple of years. By 2009, we weren't in a high-stress mode anymore. That felt good. Every day, it felt like things around us were stabilizing more and more, and we were building traction that we knew would pay off in the future. For the first time in almost two years, we relaxed enough to lift our heads out of the trenches and take a look at the rest of our industry.

It was a totally different landscape than what we had seen before the crash.

This is when we knew we were one of the only surviving shops. Investors were back, and they were hungry. The playing field was essentially completely clear for us to run the ball all the way to the end zone. There was no opposition to block our path.

That wasn't *exactly* true; the field was littered with small-time players trying to hit the opportunity presented by the low housing prices, but they weren't on our level. They didn't have our systems and processes. They didn't have great people like the employees who had stuck with us even when things got dark. They wouldn't last.

But neither would this opportunity. How could we seize it and make the most of being so well-positioned at such a unique time?

Jason and I also took a long view of the situation; sure, we could strike while the iron was hot and cash in, but we weren't in this for a short-term payday. We hadn't fought as hard as we did for those eighteen months of scraping by just to yield a windfall and get out. We wanted to build a company that would last.

I thought back to the boiler room, where I'd learned a lot of what I knew about real estate. It didn't take me long to figure out that coming up in a pre-crash, hog-wild housing market hadn't exactly set me up to crush the business game. To make the most of the opportunity in front of me, I needed to learn how to be the best entrepreneur I could be.

Luckily, learning is something I've never had trouble with. (Well, at least learning of the *entrepreneurial* kind. It did take me five and a half years to finish college, after all.)

GOING TO SCHOOL

I didn't *literally* go back to school (because talk about a waste of time). But I did create a curriculum of the best places to soak up entrepreneurial and business acumen. I attacked it in every spare moment I had.

My curriculum didn't just involve reading books and talking to experts—like the way I'd picked the brain of any willing real estate industry veteran in my early days. I found that I could learn a lot from a book, and I could pick up some great tips and advice by taking an industry elder out to lunch. But when I joined Entrepreneurs Organization (EO) and started going to every event and conference I could, that cracked open a whole new level of knowledge.

With people who had been in business for themselves, at least a few years longer than I had, I traded stories about the on-the-ground struggles we were going through. We asked each other questions: "Hey, you said you've already hired a COO. How did you know you were at that point, and how did you find one?" It was like having my own experiences multiplied out across hundreds of other entrepreneurs, reflecting back tons of ideas and ways of thinking that hadn't occurred to me.

No MBA could have delivered the massive payout I could get by investing my time in learning from other entrepreneurs like me.

The biggest benefit I got was the mindset that would carry me through the next decade at PropertyForce: that the business was bigger than just me. To truly allow my business to scale, I needed to work *on* it, not *in* it. It was an independent organism that needed to be able to operate at its top potential without Jason and me at its center. It needed to be able to thrive just as well if either of us left it.

That was a far cry from the all-hands-on-deck, every-waking-hour lifestyle Jason and I had been living throughout the recession, and it took some getting used to. But by committing to separating ourselves from the essential operation of the business, we were laying the foundations of a company that could truly take off.

LESSON #7: LEARN AND EXECUTE

I see them all the time, and I'm sure you've seen them too. These are the people who bounce around from conference to conference, networking group to networking group, event to event.

They're always there, ready to learn—but when it's time to trade stories about what's happening back at the office, they suspiciously don't have much to say. That's because they're soaking up all the incredible knowledge they can. But they're not *doing* anything with it. And their businesses go nowhere.

It's not enough to have a thirst for knowledge. It's not even enough to pursue it in every corner of the learning world; and there are a *lot* of corners. There are so many opportunities to learn that you could basically teach yourself a masterclass in entrepreneurship.

You have to *do something* with what you learn.

It's a mistake to think that attending a conference or a mastermind group is the same as doing the work. It's just not.

Start with being open to learning. Never assume that you know everything or even *most* things. Put yourself in a position to learn, and be around other people who can teach you; don't let your ego get in the way.

Then put what you learn into action. Well, put some things into action—only what makes sense for your business. You need to be selective, pace yourself, and know when to say no. That's because if you try to do everything, you'll either do nothing, or you'll send your business into multiple directions at once.

After every event I went to, every book I read, every group I talked to, I took the time to turn the knowledge and ideas I'd gained into an action plan. I'd write down three actions I could take *right now*, based on what I'd learned, and three bigger ideas for the future that I could think about over the long term. It's a simple step, but it's a step I saw other people fail to take. They didn't bring anything they learned back to their business. They got stuck in the mindset that the learning itself was the work.

At the end of the day, learning is nothing without implementation and execution. Would you rather be the guy who knows a ton about being an entrepreneur or the guy who actually, you know, *is one*?

I know which one I'd rather be—and which one I *am*.

You know who else I am? I'm the guy who learns in a group of like-minded individuals, not by only taking, but by contributing. Tell your peers what's going on at your office and what works and what doesn't. They challenge and motivate you, and they'll inspire improvements. You'll have more material you can sort through and potentially use to execute, take risks, and test, when you put it into practice.

CHAPTER EIGHT

EXPLOSIVE GROWTH

Take a look back at Lesson #3 in this book: *there's no such thing as risk-free success.*

After Jason and I had climbed our way out of the recession years and laid the solid foundations of a business that would scale for years to come, we were faced with our next big hurdle: just *how fast* should we grow?

Business started becoming easier and easier to find. Investors were finding *us*. We were booming, and we had the team, the systems, and the processes in place to turn the boom into explosive growth.

Of course, it would involve taking risks. You know we were okay with this. By now, we'd been through enough of the up-and-down cycle of business, that we were resilient. We were prepared to do what was needed in the upturn to be able to ride out the next downturn.

As I mentioned before, there's no such thing as risk-free success.

FOUR OFFICES: MORE THAN FOUR TIMES THE WORK

When Meridian Trust started skyrocketing post-recovery, the obvious next step was to expand to a second office. After all, there are only so many properties in one geographical area, and with a second office, we could double our potential inventory. It was a risk but not a huge one. Fort Lauderdale was doing *so* well that we knew we could translate the same processes to success in a new market.

We opened Office number two in Miami in 2011. It was wildly successful, pretty much immediately, a total home run. We were elated that such a big risk had paid such a huge dividend so quickly.

It wasn't without its pain points though. First of all, Jason and I barely knew what we were doing with one office, let alone two, let alone an office in a city that wasn't our own stomping grounds. One of the hard lessons we soon learned was that our systems wouldn't work exactly the same way, in a new location, as they had in Fort Lauderdale. Although business came flooding in the Miami doors, we weren't set up to handle it as well as we would have liked. Because of that, we definitely missed some opportunities.

In our first year, when we were just getting our business legs under us, this setback might have caused us to freeze. It has happened to too many other entrepreneurs: opportunities begin hitting like lightning; and with all the options that open up, it's common to freak out and stand still.

But this seemed like a *good* set of problems to have. We knew that we could make it through. We just needed to refine what we were doing in Miami and then keep moving forward.

In a way, the gaps we experienced early on in Miami forced us to up our game. We had to figure out ways to stay just as effective even while running an operation in two different cities. Our systems like marketing and HR worked well for one office, but it turned out replicating them for two wasn't as easy as we'd anticipated, so there was a ton of shoring-up that needed to happen to our processes there as well.

It made us do the work. We had to put the time in to get our shit together and make our business processes *incredibly* tight. Another thing we needed to change, now that Jason and I were in different cities, was our day-to-day communication process.

Miami forced us to be *better.* And once we got there, we kept moving forward.

Using our new, improved business operations systems, we opened a location in Tampa, in 2012, and one in Orlando, in 2013.

I can't say those expansions were 100 percent smooth, but the important part was that we didn't sit still. Knowing we'd be able to build the processes we needed to make it work, we pushed our growth forward. We jumped and built our parachute on the way down.

We combined our confidence in our resilience with careful planning and risk. Risk doesn't *negate* planning. They go hand in hand.

LESSON #8: PERFECT IS THE ENEMY OF GOOD

When we opened our Miami office, the difficulty and the work required for running an office weren't the only things that multiplied—our business and our opportunities also exploded.

With the massive influx of not only new business but also new variables, we often felt like we were trying to look in twenty different directions at once. *Look over here! No, over here! Look at this awesome thing! Hey, don't forget about this!*

By far, the most important thing we did in that crucial growth period was to *totally* detach from the idea of perfection. If we'd been obsessed with perfecting new elements of the business, before launching them, we'd never have opened the Miami office and taken advantage of that location at a time when the market was so incredibly hot. We could have played it safe, sticking with the one business in Fort Lauderdale, but instead we went for the risk; and it paid off.

When we opened the new office, I moved to Miami, which I'd always wanted to do. In the past, nothing but fear had kept me from actually doing it. I had spent so much time calculating the pros and cons that I couldn't get out of my own way. It wasn't until the office opened that I was forced into a decision.

This particular fear I had felt is known as analysis paralysis, and I see a lot of people fall prey to it. Here's why it's so common: you have ideas, opinions, opportunities, and risks constantly coming at you, from every direction, in your business and life, both from media and from people you know. With so much firing at you, it can be scary to pick one direction and go after it. What if you get it wrong?

Well, hell, big deal. So what if you heard all that and you took a risk anyway? And so what if you got it wrong? Nobody died! And you'll probably get the next one right.

The analysis-paralyzed entrepreneur never gets unstuck. His business is going nowhere.

Anyone looking to do something new is, by definition, going to do something imperfectly. Make sure you ask yourself what's the worst thing that could happen if you try the thing you're thinking of doing and you fail. Think about and write out possible outcomes, and I can almost guarantee you'll realize that they're not as bad as you thought.

Anyway, the upside if you get it right will almost always outweigh the risk of a downside. Also trust that you can recover from a mistake but not the regret you're likely to feel for not seizing the opportunity. So also ask yourself what will happen if you do nothing.

Mistakes and failure are often far less damaging than standing still.

I'll never claim that Jason and I didn't make a ton of mistakes in those years of explosive growth. There's no *way* we didn't. I'll say it again: there's no such thing as risk-free success.

But we focused on good, not perfect, and on moving forward, not staying in place. We trusted in our own proven resilience. We allowed ourselves to take leaps and figure out the *how* as we went.

It was the biggest factor in our growth. Perfection isn't the point—*progress* is. Take a shot, and fail forward!

CHAPTER NINE

ONE VISION

Hunger's important. Resilience is even more important. But there's one thing that can make or break a business partnership, especially if it's not aligned: *vision*.

Jason and I had started Meridian Trust with a singular vision. To live up to the game we'd talked in our twenties, about starting a baller company and getting rich, we'd planned our whole thirties around the business. We were going to stay single—no weddings, no kids. Guys we knew who had married young had reduced their risk tolerance to the point where they were basically handcuffed to the cushy jobs that provided for their families. We didn't knock that life, but we didn't want any part of it.

But no one was depending on us, so *we* were going to lean into risk. And we were going to keep our lives as risk-sustainable as possible. We would build a business that would scale to way more than just a steady paycheck.

It was an airtight plan. We were both all in. Until, of course, life happened.

"We're getting married," Jason told me over the phone one day, telling me he'd proposed to his girlfriend.

With any other friend, this news would have been cause for breaking out the cigars. But this wasn't *any other* friend. This was my business partner, who was supposed to ride out his thirties with me, growing the business and wealth of our dreams.

Jason's vision had changed. Now he was all in on getting married and starting a family. He was tired of the stress and uncertainty; he wanted to settle down.

"Look, the company is profitable, and we're doing great," he said. "Let's just enjoy it."

This was *not* what I was thinking at that moment. Meridian Trust was hitting a rapid growth phase, and business was exploding. I'd just amassed a huge amount of knowledge on how to scale and calculate smart risks. I wanted nothing more than to keep innovating. I had *no interest* in slowing down.

Around that time, I had also hired a business coach. She helped me sketch out my life and the business three years into the future. She had me create *my* vision of everything about Meridian Trust, down to what my office would look like.

It didn't take much coaching to see that my vision was completely different from Jason's, in a way that wouldn't work for our partnership. I wanted to accelerate the growth of the business, push it into the big leagues. I knew Jason would never get on board with my growth strategy or the systems I was trying to build.

The more I worked with my coach, the easier it was to see a truth I'd resisted: Jason and I now had different visions, and the partnership was no longer going to work out.

When I brought this truth to Jason, it didn't seem like that much of a surprise to him. He'd already come to essentially the same conclusion. He was ready to take necessary steps. The obvious route was that I buy him out.

It might have been obvious, but it took me nearly a year to come to the ultimate decision: that I needed to put up the money to do it. It was a huge decision, one of the biggest of my life—even more so because buying Jason out meant putting up a *lot* of money. It was a big deal.

That wasn't even the biggest factor in the difficulty of my

decision, though. Jason had been the operations half of our partnership. Did I have what I would need to run a company on the ground? Would I have time to keep scaling the company *while* taking on Jason's side of the partnership?

Was I about to take on too much and cripple the company?

This is where risk comes back into the equation. It was a definite risk to take over operations and fully own all sides of the business. But after months of agonizing back-and-forth—while Jason and I risked losing our friendship forever—I came to the only conclusion I could see.

It was him or me.

To this day, Jason is one of my best friends. It was one of the hardest things I've ever done to walk into his office and lay out an ultimatum: "One of us has to go. I'm okay with you buying me out, but I'd prefer to buy you out. Let's do this."

After I said it, there was no going back.

Four weeks of intense negotiation later, he walked away with the money, and I walked away with PropertyForce.

LESSON #9: LONG-TERM CHANGE COMES FROM SHORT-TERM STEPS

The lesson I learned through the business "divorce" I went through was simple: vision is everything. There's no road forward with diverging visions. Jason and I realized that we had fundamentally different perceptions of what we wanted for the future and of what our business could and should be.

A successful business *has* to have one cohesive vision. The founders have to share that vision—and if they ever fall out of sync, they need to get back on the same page immediately.

The work I did to come to this conclusion didn't start with thinking about splitting with my business partner at all. It started with simply thinking about my long-term goals. The more I worked with my business coach to envision what I wanted from my future, the more it became clear that the situation I was in had to change.

To get to where I wanted to go in three years, or even five years, I had to eliminate the immediate roadblock to my long-term goal. I had to map out the short-term steps that would move me closer to it.

Long-term goals are uncomfortable to think about; they seem huge, like climbing a mountain. But if you take the time to map out what short-term steps you need to take to get there, you'll see that the journey of a thousand miles really does begin with a single step.

This goes for anything you do in life, not just business. You need to make short-term changes to reach your long-term goals. Start with envisioning what you want your future to be in three or five years, then write out that vision as if you're already there. *Then* take it down to a one-year outlook. Break down what you need to accomplish in every quarter. The other key is to behave, every day, like the person you'll be when you achieve your long-term goals. Take on the daily activities of that future self of yours.

If *you* ever find yourself in the middle of splitting with your business partner, I think you'll also be grateful for this lesson I learned: a business split doesn't have to be a shit show or a battle. In the end, our deal meant that Jason would get the stability he wanted, with the time to spend with his family and enough money to never have to work again. I would get the decision-making power I needed to go after the dream my business coach had shown me was possible.

With those fundamental needs met, it was just a matter of drawing up terms. Having come up together, buying and selling properties, Jason and I both knew that a successful negotiation means both parties have to leave something on the table. You can't get hung up on winning or losing. If you do it the right way, you can even stay friends.

We did it the right way. After four brutal weeks, we settled on a number, shook hands, and it was all over.

We were friends again.

We drew up paperwork, Jason stayed on for a few months to help me with the transition, and that was that. I was on my own.

I don't think that Jason and I would have remained close friends if we'd ignored reality and stayed in an unworkable situation longer than we did. It was a painful decision, no doubt. But the bigger risk to the company would have been ignoring the writing on the wall and staying together. It would have killed the company.

In the end, an entrepreneur's top priority isn't friendship, it isn't partnership, and it isn't stability.

It's the future.

If something or someone in your life—a partner, job, spouse, whatever—doesn't align with your vision, it's time to make a change. It might take you out of your comfort zone, and it might be difficult and come with extra work in the short term. But it will all be worth it, and you'll feel good, because you're living your truth.

CHAPTER TEN

CHANGE

THE GOOD, THE BAD, AND THE UGLY

I'd be lying if I said that, once the buyout was over, every-thing went back to normal.

But I'd also be lying if I described a long period of turbu-lence and dust-settling. Things were different, sure, but the company was still doing great. In fact, right after the buyout, we posted our highest earnings ever.

We barely had any competition, all four of our offices were rock-solid and profitable, and our systems were dialed in to a point where other companies were looking to *us* for direction—we were leading the way.

During this time, I threw myself into running the operations side of the company. To be able to lead my company forward, I needed to understand every piece of it. I couldn't outsource any responsibility until I'd learned and mastered it myself.

The huge investment I'd made into the buyout—financially, operationally, and emotionally—had paid off big-time. I couldn't have been happier.

So of course, this was the moment I chose to make a move that sent everything straight to hell in a matter of weeks.

RIPPING OFF THE BAND-AID

In the middle of 2015, I got antsy.

As I mentioned, business almost couldn't have been better. I'd had a taste of my ideas and careful strategizing paying off, and I was feeling a little high on myself, honestly. I was more than confident—I was a little cocky.

Don't get me wrong. Cocky's not *bad*. It's just risky. And in this case, the risk was one that it didn't even occur to me to calculate.

Along with our four main offices, we had remote agents scattered throughout the state. There were constant management and personnel issues. Those of us on the executive team were constantly traveling between the main offices to put out fires and get things back in line, which was a big drain on our time. It was like playing a constant game of whack-a-mole. And our agents had to fill a lot of different roles, which meant they weren't working as efficiently as they could.

Business was great, but how much better could it be if we tightened up our processes? Were we succeeding *in spite of* ourselves, rather than because of our hard work?

My mind kept coming back to a central question that kept me up some nights: *how can I scale this business even faster?*

Throughout the life of the business, I'd been bootstrapping our growth with my own ideas, stuff I'd learned from attending mastermind groups and EO, reading books, and personally surveying industry vets. But now it occurred to me that fresh eyes could help me see even more ways to improve, so for the first time, I brought in a consultant.

I'd been playing around with a pretty radical idea. It would mean completely overhauling our systems, but the potential ROI was massive. It would literally bring the company into the future and set us up for the next decade or longer.

My consultant agreed with me—it was exactly the kind of innovation that launches an already-successful business into the stratosphere.

He pushed me to be even more aggressive than was normal for me (which is saying a lot—in case you haven't noticed, on a *slow* day, I'm around an eight on a ten-point aggressiveness scale). He advised me to rip off the Band-Aid and change everything at once, so the company could continue moving forward, but aligned in a new process.

So that's what I did.

I shut down all four offices in a week and brought all forty employees to a single location between our former Miami and Lauderdale offices. Together, we completely changed the way we do business. The sweeping changes applied to everything from tech to client management, and the company looked completely different on the other end. What we did was to take the business completely virtual. This "virtual wholesale" model would later be copied by others in the industry, but we're the ones who pioneered it.

While we doubled down on better systems and processes, with technology as the centerpiece, we rebranded the company as PropertyForce. Starting to look at the company as more of a technology and marketing company was good in some ways. But at the end of the day, the company was, still is, and always will be a sales company at the core.

Naturally, this transformation led to some pandemonium. I expected it. But I didn't expect total *chaos*.

To say that this was a difficult time for both the business and me would be a huge understatement. Things got *dark*.

The biggest problem was the effect of combining our Miami and Fort Lauderdale offices, our two largest. They had been only about a thirty-minute drive from each other, so it seemed like an obvious move to make. But each office had its own mini-culture, and we didn't do a good job of integrating the people in them. When we combined them in one space, it was a classic "one bad apple spoils the bunch" situation. A couple of toxic people, who could be managed more easily in smaller groups, suddenly became a much bigger issue.

I'm not talking about just water-cooler talk or bad work ethic. We caught people *stealing* from the company and outright *violating* their noncompete agreements.

I had to take them to court, and it wasn't fun. These were people I'd hired and worked with, who'd been part of the company in good times and bad. I was totally on the defensive, though, motivated to protect my turf. I had never been litigious or had to take anyone to court for anything significant. But I felt like I had to do it to protect the business.

I won every lawsuit and took down six people in the process. It was a victory. But I didn't feel victorious.

LESSON #10: NOT EVERYONE THINKS LIKE YOU

I'm a guy who rolls with the punches. Hell, I actually *like* the punches.

Change doesn't faze me. Sure, change can be painful, but the pain is worth it, because I know it almost always gets you somewhere better on the other end. Anyway, I have a high pain tolerance.

But here's a hard lesson I learned when I changed everything about our business in one fell swoop: *not everyone thinks like me.*

I introduced the changes with massive excitement, and everyone was hyped; everyone was game.

That didn't mean everyone was *ready.*

It hadn't occurred to me that the sweeping changes would hit other people differently and that not everyone had the same tolerance for rolling with the punches. My biggest mistake was forgetting about the human element in a business decision. Every business decision *always* involves people, and to forget that fact is to dig a hole you can't easily climb out of.

In addition to the lawsuits, this new hole I found myself

in included resignations and what would amount to an 80 percent turnover in 2016, the year after the big change.

Now, looking back, was the decision to rip the Band-Aid off and change the business model *wrong?* No. *Hell* no. In fact, I ended up being completely right about all the ROI the change would reap over the coming years.

I'm also proud of having pioneered virtual wholesale. It brought challenges, stress, and a lot of upfront cost, but I would not have traded it for the satisfaction and the more tactile rewards of innovating!

But I do regret that I forgot about change *management.* And it still stings that many of the hard lessons I learned were things I already knew. I thought the transition would be easy, so in a week of stupidity, I skipped steps I knew were important. That's because I was thinking about the changes only in the context of what *I felt* and how they would affect me personally.

If you want to be a pioneer, at the end of the day, you have to be prepared for the challenges, good and bad, that come with your new world. Not everyone will be on board with the changes you make, no matter how carefully you intro-duce them. If you *are* careful and *still* get people who oppose them, be prepared to cut bait with them and focus on nurturing relationships with your supporters. (This also applies to changes you make in your *life*, not just your business.)

These days, I don't make a single decision without considering its impact on the people I lead and carefully managing any change so that people feel supported. People are the most important part of any business, and they're not robots. Their perspectives are unique. A surefire way to piss *everyone* off is to ignore that uniqueness, change their whole world overnight, and expect them to roll with the punches.

They'll punch back.

CHAPTER ELEVEN

BACK ON MY FEET

When the massive changes I made to the business nearly tanked everything, I knew I could get through it. Again, that old confidence in my resilience came out.

But I also knew I couldn't do it alone. If I'd learned anything from the rough patches I'd endured in my business and in my life, it was that I needed a team of experts to rely on for advice. I didn't have to figure out the way forward by myself.

At the beginning of 2017, I started working with a new business coach who helped me see some areas where I'd been behind the eight ball. I'd initially tried to hire him as PropertyForce's COO, but he didn't bite. He taught me about the basics of business that I'd overlooked and outsourced before. I'm talking the nitty-gritty stuff: unit economics, P&L management, and change management. Getting a handle on it now helped me to level up not only the business but also myself as an entrepreneur.

He also helped me see something obvious: I needed to get myself *out* of the day-to-day aspects of the business as much as possible.

Especially after Jason departed, I'd tightened my grip on the day-to-day operations of the business. Part of this was just needing to know how it was done; Jason had filled that role before, and if I was ever going to be able to offload duties to a COO, I needed to be an expert in the operational side myself. For the second time, I had to be in the operational side of the business. I had learned to operate in the Meridian Trust environment, but I had to figure out the operations of the new virtual environment of PropertyForce before I could offload them.

But all that decision-making and hands-on work was keeping me from doing what I did best: create the broader vision for the company. If I had focused on that earlier, it definitely would have helped me identify the change-management gaps that had proved so catastrophic to the business.

My business coach helped me understand how to do what I'd always wanted to do: scale the business faster. Having come from a COO background, he helped me see things tactically and understand what good operational decisions look like. These revelations took some pressure off, and I was able to get back, somewhat, to what I do best.

The results were immediate. Suddenly the business was growing like crazy, and I was ecstatic.

I'd been backed into a corner several times. I'd seen things go incredibly well only to see them fall apart months later. After a long, crazy road—splitting with my business partner, followed by rampant growth, followed by poorly-managed change that nearly spelled the end of everything—I finally felt like I was back on my feet.

The funny thing was, almost none of my problems had been with the business itself. The business had been going *great*— for a long time. Even the changes to the business model I'd made were setting us up to hit it out of the park in the next decade; we were ahead of the curve in so many ways, and it was paying off hugely.

All my problems were simply due to my own mistakes, simply due to a lack of experience that led to poor decisions. In a weird way, that was a relief. After all, if they were my mistakes, I was in total control of fixing them. I had everything I needed to do so—the willingness to learn, experts and peers to ask for help, and the resilience to bounce back from change.

By 2018 the business wasn't just thriving; it was hitting

numbers I'd barely dreamed of. I'd put the foundations in place to keep the ride smooth while we continued to grow and expand. I'd even avoided my own burnout by taking what I'd learned from my new business coach and offloading operational duties to good and competent people. I had my brother Robert co-running the sales floor with Jason, a staff member who had stuck with me through all of the good and bad. I had Carlos as my right-hand person, and my top agent was Jordan, a close friend of twenty years. The four of them did a great job of running things and helping me through all of the changes in the company. More importantly, I could trust them. They were part of the fabric of the company and had its best interest, and mine, at heart. They would be able to give me great feedback at the ground level.

Things were looking up. With a feeling of relief and satisfaction, because I knew PropertyForce was in good hands, I took off for a ten-day trip to Europe with my college buddies, a trip I look forward to every year. For the first time in years, I didn't have a nagging sense of worry as the plane hit cruising altitude.

LESSON #11: TAKE ADVANTAGE OF COACHING

The biggest lesson I learned during this period wasn't anything new or revolutionary. It wasn't a new process or system. It also wasn't a tip from one of my business masterminds. And it didn't require me digging deep into my innate resiliency.

This lesson was simple: *don't try to be everything*. Ask for and accept help.

You *can't* be everything all at once, and for a time, after the shakeup of the business change, that's what I was trying to be. I was trying to be the visionary *and* the operational mind in the business, and I was heading straight toward burnout. It doesn't matter what you're dealing with in life—you can't play all roles at once, and if you try, you won't play any of them really well.

Getting a strong understanding of your strengths and weaknesses is important not only as an ego exercise but as a way to avoid trying to be everything to everyone. Recognize that not everything that needs to happen needs to be done *by you* specifically. I went out and found someone who could help me with the aspects of the business I was weak at, and it allowed me to focus more on where I really shine.

You *can* learn to do many different things. But you can only do one or two things *excellently*. Focus in on those things, and offload the rest.

After the major shakeups and ugly personal battles of the business change, all I needed to do to get back on track was trust what had already worked for me. I went back to what I knew. I took the time to recover—I didn't rush it. I allowed the knowledge that I had worked through serious challenges to guide me through this latest one.

A big part of the mistakes I'd made, in consolidating offices and changing our business model, was *rushing*. I'd skipped steps. I'd gone too fast, impatient to see the ROI from all the work.

But when it came to righting the ship, I was methodical. I carefully considered everything that needed to be stabilized, got advice from my coach and my team on how to do it, and put changes in place one at a time.

I also took *very* seriously the thoughts and feedback of my employees. Losing sight of what they were feeling and experiencing with the business changes had bitten me on the ass hard; I wouldn't make that mistake again.

As an entrepreneur, or anyone who wants to challenge the status quo to create a better life, you have to know you're going to make mistakes. You're going to mess up hugely sometimes.

Those mistakes don't erase everything you've done *right*. And they don't mean you don't know what you're doing. Trust your intuition, and what has worked for you. Just because your problem is new doesn't mean the solution has to be. And call for help when you need it. No matter what it costs, hire the best person—whether a consultant, a coach, or a friend—in the area that's causing you trouble.

CHAPTER TWELVE

YOU CAN'T BE EVERYTHING

BUT YOU ALSO CAN'T BE *NOTHING*

We'd been tracking our progress and celebrating our achievements as a company every quarter since we had enough employees to qualify for the term "all-hands." But the all-hands meeting we held at the end of the second quarter of 2018 was a true moment of triumph. This quarter was our biggest ever in terms of revenue and profit. We were flying high, and we were all *pumped*.

Especially after the rough patch we'd just come through, the feeling of finally being out of the woods was absolutely incredible. I felt that my team had really *bought in*. They weren't just showing up for their jobs. They had committed to being on a winning team, and they were enthusiastic about how they spent their days.

That's another reason why, when I left for Europe, I felt secure knowing my company was in great hands. With plans to check in with my business coach and COO regularly, I let go for probably the first time in years. I relaxed.

I spent four days in Israel, then went to Sweden, where I watched the quarter-finals of the World Cup on TV. England had beaten Sweden and would face Croatia in the semifinals in Moscow, which I'd been dying to visit. What's more, my family is from England, and Croatia is my favorite country in the world (I've been there more than ten times!). I took all that as a sign that I needed to go to Moscow, and I heeded it.

In Russia, I met up with my dad and other friends and saw the World Cup. I had a return ticket home, but then some *more* friends invited me to stay with them in the house they'd rented in Croatia in a month. It would mean either leaving Europe and coming back or extending the trip.

I checked in with the business. Both my business coach and my COO presented a unified front: "It's fine! Everything's great! This is a good exercise for you to relinquish some control. We got it!"

I allowed myself to believe them. To be fair, I didn't have any reason not to. Looking back, though, I should have asked more questions.

I extended the trip from Russia to Greece, Italy, France, Switzerland, and Poland and finally ended up in Croatia. Ten days became three weeks became two months. It was the most freedom I could remember feeling since I'd started a business; I just went where the wind took me and had a blast.

When I got home, I found an absolute disaster zone waiting for me.

I landed in Florida on a Sunday, and the moment I stepped back into the office the next day, I could tell that *everything* had changed. The entire vibe felt off. People looked miserable. Hell, even the *air* felt different.

And if I thought the people looked miserable, seeing the books felt like a bucket of freezing cold water thrown over me. Just my first glance at the numbers showed me that, in as little as seven weeks, our revenue had *tanked*.

I was in disbelief. How could this have *happened*? Why had my proxies whom I'd left in charge reassured me that everything was fine, when it *clearly* wasn't?

It was such a mountain of shit that I literally couldn't handle it at first. One of my best friends was getting married that month, and I was throwing the bachelor party in Vegas that weekend. I got right back on a plane on Wednesday and ran away from the whole situation.

I'd never considered myself someone who avoided his problems, but I'd never been faced with a total implosion of this magnitude.

By the time the weekend ended, though, reality had set in. I knew the truth of what had happened: I'd taken my finger off the pulse of my business. I hadn't just gotten myself out of the operations; I'd completely ignored them. I needed to get back to Florida and, one more time, right the ship.

LESSON #12: HIT THE RIGHT BALANCE

There's no doubt about it: PropertyForce hit its roughest patch yet, because of my own mistake.

I had already started to see slight cracks in the business, within the first two weeks of my trip to Europe, but I convinced myself that I had the measures and controls in place to keep everything running smoothly while I was gone. But we were in an aggressive growth stage, and in it, the slightest step off course can quickly become a huge swing in the wrong direction. I should have listened to my instincts.

I could try to point the finger at the people I left at the helm, while I was in Europe, but it wouldn't be fair at all. The truth was, they were *very* capable of running the company—at the size and business volume it had been back in 2016–2017. But by 2018, we'd leveled up to such an enormous extent that they couldn't handle operations on their own. The business didn't need me tangled up in the minute-by-minute operations; but the opposite—my being totally absent—was far worse. I didn't strike a balance; I swung from one extreme to the other, from doing *everything* to doing *nothing*.

I took my finger off the pulse of the company. I got complacent. I thought I'd fought through the hardest fight I'd ever have to endure, but I was dead wrong.

This was a lesson I took hard. Not only had I been disappointed by people I thought I could rely on, but I hadn't set them up for success in the first place, and it spelled catastrophe for the people who relied on *me*.

At the end of the day it was my business. The responsibility fell to me. I should have seen that—and I should have been more involved. I could have gone on a ten-day trip, and things would have been fine. But I swung to the extreme and spent two months away. That was too long.

I had underestimated how much the business needed me, and I promised never to make that mistake again. Even now, while I've removed myself from much of the day-to-day operations, I still go into the office. When I don't, things fall through the cracks.

But that's the role of the visionary. I see the things that other people don't see, and I own everything, both the good and the bad. You can't delegate that out. You also can't delegate inspiration. When I'm there, our team operates at a different level than they do when I'm gone.

As a friend of mine once said to me, "When you own a business, when everything's good, you're on top of the world. When it's bad, the world is on top of you."

That's absolutely what it felt like after my two-month trip. And the worst part was, I'd put myself there. If there was ever a time for my resilience to help me get back off the ropes, this was it. I truly believe that the difference between someone who achieves major success in life and someone who doesn't is resilience. Business tends to come in waves. You have two good years and a horrendous year—or the reverse.

How much can you stomach? How much can you really push through? If you can get through it, learn from it, and apply those lessons to the next round, you're good.

If you can't, you fail. For me, failure was *not* an option. I had worked too hard, overcome too many obstacles, and had too many people relying on me.

Just as I was to blame for what happened, it now fell to me to get my company back on track.

Over the past few years, and again at the end of that long trip, I have learned a lot about balance. For one thing, I found out that the reason you become unbalanced is because you tend to neglect one area of your life in favor of a heavy focus on another. The key is to maintain moderation in all the important components of life—business and finance, health, social and community, fun, spiritualism, family, relationships—and not go to extremes in any one, or you'll ignore another.

CHAPTER THIRTEEN

YOU'RE NOT ALONE

If that previous chapter led you to believe that things aren't great in my world, think again.

True, it was a bitter pill to swallow; I'd brought my company back from an incredibly disruptive change in our business model, only to see it crash around my feet again when I ignored my instincts and stayed in Europe for weeks. And true, digging myself out of the hole I found my company in, when I got back, was the biggest obstacle I've ever had to face in business.

But I'll always circle back to the one thing I *know* about myself: that deep-down resiliency I've always had in spades. I knew rebuilding PropertyForce, after my disaster of a sabbatical, would be tough. But I also knew I could do it.

And I did.

In the two years since I returned from that long overseas trip, I brought my company back from rock bottom because I took the time to invest in, grow, and support the right people to help me rebuild. I started with the simplest thing I could think of: I talked to every person one-on-one.

Sitting down with each person in the company, face-to-face, and simply listening to what they had to say was probably the biggest-impact action I've taken as an entrepreneur. Not only did it allow me to see everyone's individual perspective, I came out of those meetings with a giant list of problems I could attack. I isolated the different types of problems and started knocking them out one by one.

I got super hands-on as I dove into the nitty-gritty of running the business, taking over the sales floor, and putting all the pieces in place to scale nationally.

By the time I'd fixed the biggest foundational issues, I was ready to do what I'd never been able to do before: build a true executive team. I assumed the roles of president and CEO (today I'm the CEO, and have brought in a seasoned president). Then I struck a chord of balance through delegation, not abdication. I brought on a head of marketing, head of sales, and controller. Now I'm looking for a head of systems and operations.

For the first time, I wasn't alone running the business; it wasn't all on me, and I could really trust that, in my absence, the company wouldn't fall apart. I'd done what I'd been trying to do for years: build a company that could thrive and scale, even if I wasn't watching every part of it every minute of the day.

It was a huge step forward for my life. And it was a huge *leap* forward for the company. With the empowerment and trust to run things on their own, everyone at PropertyForce leveled up in their skills and development. It took my letting go of control to see that, if you invest in putting the right people in the right seats and help them grow, you'll all get to the next level together.

At this point, you've seen the biggest lessons I had to learn as I navigated achieving success as an entrepreneur. Every one of those lessons is important, and without everything that's happened to me, I can honestly say that I wouldn't be the man I am today.

If there's one thread of commonality that runs through all those lessons, it's this: you have to take a leap of faith. And you have to trust that your resilience will land you on your feet.

That's true of life too. Life is a series of leaps of faith. You see an opportunity, you jump to reach it, and you build your parachute as you fall. None of us get anywhere by standing still—we're all moving through life, calculating risk, and deciding when to jump.

Looking back on my whole story, I can also see another key thread that ties it together.

People.

Through all the good times and bad and all the ups and downs, I wasn't alone. I had the benefit of a great team of people who stuck with me, helped me see things I was missing, and drove my lessons home even harder.

A COMPANY OF C STUDENTS

Recently, a business coach asked me what we're looking for in an employee at PropertyForce.

I thought about it before answering: we want C students who are willing to hustle to become A players and who want to live A lives.

What are A players? They have a deep sense of their own abilities and their company's ability to succeed. They love to compete. And they're self-starters—they find a way to complete every job without complaining, procrastinating, or criticizing others. They anticipate problems, and they possess integrity, a quality that's nearly impossible to teach.

And what's an A life? It's defined in holistic, not just financial, terms. It's about work-life balance—living a life that brings you happiness, whatever that means to you.

I built PropertyForce for people like me. The company was founded by C students, and it offers a great home to people like us—people who are coachable and capable of delivering results. Stanford or Ivy League graduates aren't going to come work with us, and we're okay with that. Our C students are authentic, hardworking, and committed to growth.

We have a system that we've built up over time, and to fit into that system, you need to be willing to learn and put your ego aside. I've found that people who have been successful in sales elsewhere, or who have a lot of experience in real estate, want to do things their own way and aren't open to learning a new way of doing things. They're not open to learning, period.

What *I've* learned is that everyone is different; they have different styles and different interests, and they come from different places. But if the C students we're looking for are genuine and true to themselves, they'll do very well here.

That's the common thread that runs through all the people who work for us.

A poster in the PropertyForce office lists the ten things you don't need talent for:

1. Being on time
2. Work ethic
3. Effort
4. Body language
5. Energy
6. Attitude
7. Passion
8. Being coachable
9. Doing extra
10. Being prepared

This poster is our small way of letting people know that they are absolutely capable of building the essential traits that help people succeed in this—or any—business. You may not have a formal education, but if you're hungry and you have high emotional intelligence and street smarts, maybe you can find a home here.

YOU'RE NOT ALONE—BUT THE LEAP IS UP TO YOU

I assume you picked up this book because you want more out of your life than you have. If you want to take your life or your business to the next level, you can't keep doing what you're doing now.

If you want more, you have to give more and do it every day for a long time, even when the going gets tough.

Tony Robbins says great leadership is being anticipatory, not reactionary. As a leader at PropertyForce, I see my job as trying to see the bumps in the road before we hit them. Practicing that skill in business has translated over to my own life; I can see when something hard is coming at me and take steps to make sure it doesn't hit as hard.

That's all fine and good, but how do you learn to see those bumps? Some of it is just raw experience. I've been through some shit, I've learned from it, and I know what's likely to happen again. I can anticipate problems now that, two years ago, I wouldn't have been able to.

But even the best of us can only see so far. Nobody really sees the future—we're all traveling into the unknown. It's impossible to anticipate everything. No matter how much you prepare, you won't understand until you're in it.

Uncharted territory is tough. Expect surprises. As I sit here writing this book, we're in the middle of a global pandemic, and business—and life—are pretty much on hold. I have no idea what's going to happen, but I know that, with the right people around me and with the lessons I've talked about in this book, I'll be able to overcome whatever challenges are on the other end of this crisis.

If you want something different than you've ever known, you'll have to deal with territory you've never seen. You won't know everything it's going to take. But you'll commit to doing whatever it takes anyway.

For instance, when the market crashed, none of us predicted the full extent of the disaster or how deep the hole it would create for our business would get. But we put our heads down, stayed true to our fundamentals, and we got through it. When you're backed into a corner, if you can find your inner strength to do whatever it takes, if you can find your inner *grit*, you'll make it.

Just know that it all comes down to you.

The resources are out there. The books, the mentors, the conferences; they are available to you if you go looking. You can find everything you need.

But no one is going to do it for you.

At the end of the day, you have to rely on your own resourcefulness. Yes, you can find people to help you along the way, but it's your life. You have to take the lead. When you do, be mentally prepared for everything that's going to come.

There will always be good days and bad days. When the bad days hit, remind yourself that it's temporary and, when you get good days, *that they're only temporary.* Be prepared for that constant rise and fall, and just enjoy the ride.

Lean on other people. Ask hard questions. Keep learning and executing. But at the end of the day, there's no silver bullet.

When it comes to your life, you're the one in charge.

ABOUT THE AUTHOR

OLIVER SEIDLER is the co-founder and CEO of PropertyForce, an industry-leading real estate investment company focused on culture and employee success. After quickly becoming a top producer in real estate, Oliver started his own company in 2006. He weathered the recession and extended PropertyForce's reach outside of Florida in 2017, with future expansion plans in the works. Aside from work, Seidler mentors young businesspeople, invests in startups, and works with Boys and Girls Clubs of America. He has a master's degree in Entrepreneurship from The Birthing of Giants program at MIT and is a member of EO and YPO.

CPSIA information can be obtained
at www.ICGtesting.com
Printed in the USA
LVHW030723110721
692392LV00002B/178